# Fishing Log

# & ACTIVITY BOOK

# FOR KIDS

# FISHING CHECKLIST
Before you go, do you have everything you need?

Fishing Pole

Tackle Box

Fishing Hooks

Bobber

Bucket

Waterproof Shoes

Bait

Lunch/Snacks

# ABOUT MY FISHING TRIP

Date: __Nov. 6, 2020__

Where was it at? __Sanibel Cosway__

Who did you go with? __Grandpa, Tim, Evan__

How long did you fish? __1/2 hour__

What was the weather like? __Sunny & breezy__

How many fish did you catch? __1 fish long__
__with Elmo mouth & teeth__

What was your favorite part of the trip? _____
__Playing w/ the dead fish__
_____

What was your least favorite part? _____
__Waiting__
_____

# DRAW A PICTURE OF SOMETHING FROM YOUR TRIP:

# ABOUT MY FISHING TRIP

Date:_____

Where was it at? _____

Who did you go with?_____

How long did you fish? _____

What was the weather like? _____

How many fish did you catch?_____

What was your favorite part of the trip? _____
_____
_____

What was your least favorite part? _____
_____
_____

## FUN FISHING FACT:
THERE ARE MANY WAYS TO CATCH FISH, INCLUDING HAND GATHERING, SPEARING, NETTING, USING A POLE, AND TRAPPING.

DRAW A PICTURE OF SOMETHING FROM YOUR TRIP:

# ✑ ABOUT MY FISHING TRIP ✑

Date:_____

Where was it at? _____

Who did you go with?_____

How long did you fish? _____

What was the weather like? _____

How many fish did you catch?_____

What was your favorite part of the trip? _____

_____

_____

What was your least favorite part? _____

_____

_____

# DRAW A PICTURE OF SOMETHING FROM YOUR TRIP:

# COLOR IN THE FISHING LURES!

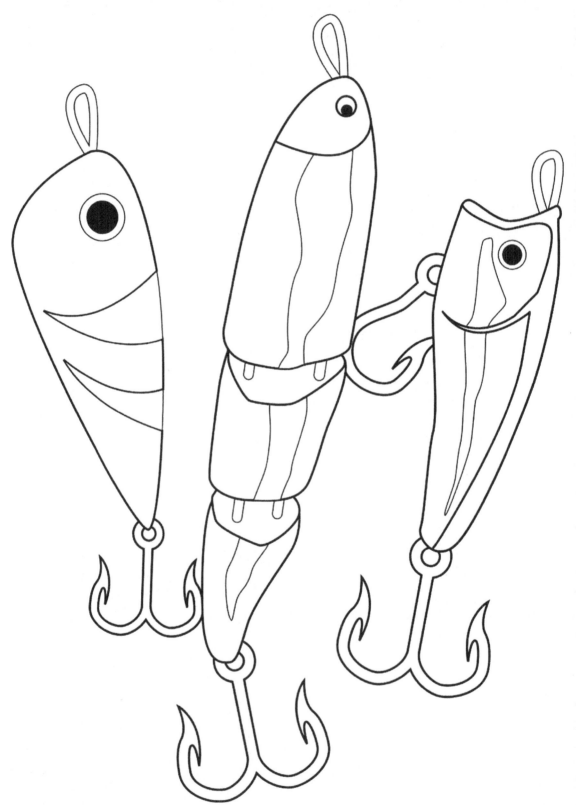

# NATURE SCAVENGER HUNT
## Circle all the things you find on the list!

Bird

Clover

Tree

Stump or Log

Flower

Cloud

Insect

Leaf

# ✠〰 ABOUT MY FISHING TRIP 〰✠

Date:_____

Where was it at? _____

Who did you go with?_____

How long did you fish? _____

What was the weather like? _____

How many fish did you catch?_____

What was your favorite part of the trip? _____

_____

_____

What was your least favorite part? _____

_____

_____

DRAW A PICTURE OF SOMETHING FROM YOUR TRIP:

# ❮⬩❭ ABOUT MY FISHING TRIP ❮⬩❭

Date:_____

Where was it at? _____

Who did you go with?_____

How long did you fish? _____

What was the weather like? _____

How many fish did you catch?_____

What was your favorite part of the trip? _____

_____

_____

What was your least favorite part? _____

_____

_____

**FUN FISHING FACT:**
SPORT FISHING IS A CONTEST WHERE
FISHERMEN TRY TO GET MORE FISH
THAN OTHER FISHERMEN.

# DRAW A PICTURE OF SOMETHING FROM YOUR TRIP:

# ABOUT MY FISHING TRIP

Date:_____

Where was it at? _____

Who did you go with?_____

How long did you fish? _____

What was the weather like? _____

How many fish did you catch?_____

What was your favorite part of the trip? _____
_____
_____

What was your least favorite part? _____
_____
_____

DRAW A PICTURE OF SOMETHING FROM YOUR TRIP:

# COLOR IN THE PICTURE!

# COLOR IN THE PICTURE!

# 🐟 ABOUT MY FISHING TRIP 🐟

Date:_____

Where was it at? _____

Who did you go with?_____

How long did you fish? _____

What was the weather like? _____

How many fish did you catch?_____

What was your favorite part of the trip? _____

_____

_____

What was your least favorite part? _____

_____

_____

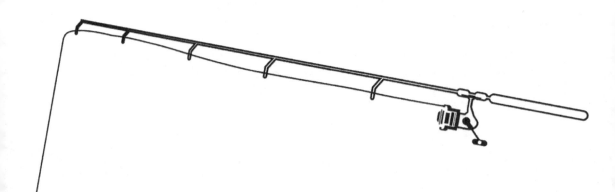

# DRAW A PICTURE OF SOMETHING FROM YOUR TRIP:

# ⊱∈⊰ ABOUT MY FISHING TRIP ⊱∈⊰

Date:_____

Where was it at? _____

Who did you go with?_____

How long did you fish? _____

What was the weather like? _____

How many fish did you catch?_____

What was your favorite part of the trip? _____

_____

_____

What was your least favorite part? _____

_____

_____

FUN FISHING FACT:

FISHING DONE WITH A FISHING ROD, LINE AND
HOOK TO GET THE FISH IS CALLED ANGLING.

DRAW A PICTURE OF SOMETHING FROM YOUR TRIP:

# ABOUT MY FISHING TRIP

Date:_____

Where was it at? _____

Who did you go with?_____

How long did you fish? _____

What was the weather like? _____

How many fish did you catch?_____

What was your favorite part of the trip? _____

_____

_____

What was your least favorite part? _____

_____

_____

DRAW A PICTURE OF SOMETHING FROM YOUR TRIP:

# COLOR IN THE PICTURE!

# MAZE

Help the fishermen get to the fish!

# ABOUT MY FISHING TRIP

Date:_____

Where was it at? _____

Who did you go with?_____

How long did you fish? _____

What was the weather like? _____

How many fish did you catch?_____

What was your favorite part of the trip? _____

_____

_____

What was your least favorite part? _____

_____

_____

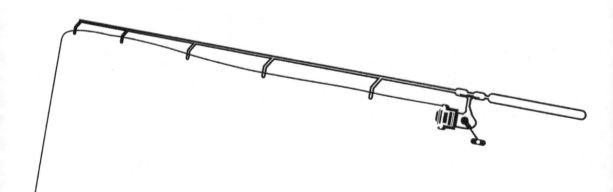

DRAW A PICTURE OF SOMETHING FROM YOUR TRIP:

# ABOUT MY FISHING TRIP

Date:_____

Where was it at? _____

Who did you go with?_____

How long did you fish? _____

What was the weather like? _____

How many fish did you catch?_____

What was your favorite part of the trip? _____

_____

_____

What was your least favorite part? _____

_____

_____

FUN FISHING FACT:

THERE ARE OVER 33,000
DIFFERENT SPECIES OF FISH!

# DRAW A PICTURE OF SOMETHING FROM YOUR TRIP:

# ABOUT MY FISHING TRIP

Date:_____

Where was it at? _____

Who did you go with?_____

How long did you fish? _____

What was the weather like? _____

How many fish did you catch?_____

What was your favorite part of the trip? _____

_____

_____

What was your least favorite part? _____

_____

_____

DRAW A PICTURE OF SOMETHING FROM YOUR TRIP:

# COLOR IN THE PICTURE OF THE LOONS!

# COLOR IN THE PICTURE!

# 🐟 ABOUT MY FISHING TRIP 🐟

Date:_____

Where was it at? _____

Who did you go with?_____

How long did you fish? _____

What was the weather like? _____

How many fish did you catch?_____

What was your favorite part of the trip? _____
_____
_____

What was your least favorite part? _____
_____
_____

DRAW A PICTURE OF SOMETHING FROM YOUR TRIP:

 ABOUT MY FISHING TRIP

Date:_____

Where was it at? _____

Who did you go with?_____

How long did you fish? _____

What was the weather like? _____

How many fish did you catch?_____

What was your favorite part of the trip? _____

_____

_____

What was your least favorite part? _____

_____

_____

FUN FISHING FACT:
FISH DON'T HAVE LUNGS, INSTEAD
THEY HAVE GILLS THAT TAKE OXYGEN
FROM THE WATER AROUND THEM.

# DRAW A PICTURE OF SOMETHING FROM YOUR TRIP:

# 🐟 ABOUT MY FISHING TRIP 🐟

Date:_____

Where was it at? _____

Who did you go with?_____

How long did you fish? _____

What was the weather like? _____

How many fish did you catch?_____

What was your favorite part of the trip? _____

_____

_____

What was your least favorite part? _____

_____

_____

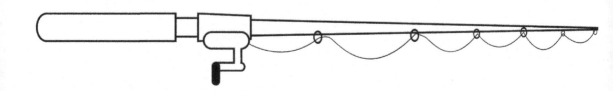

DRAW A PICTURE OF SOMETHING FROM YOUR TRIP:

# COLOR IN THE PICTURE!

# TIC TAC TOE

First to get 3 in a row wins!

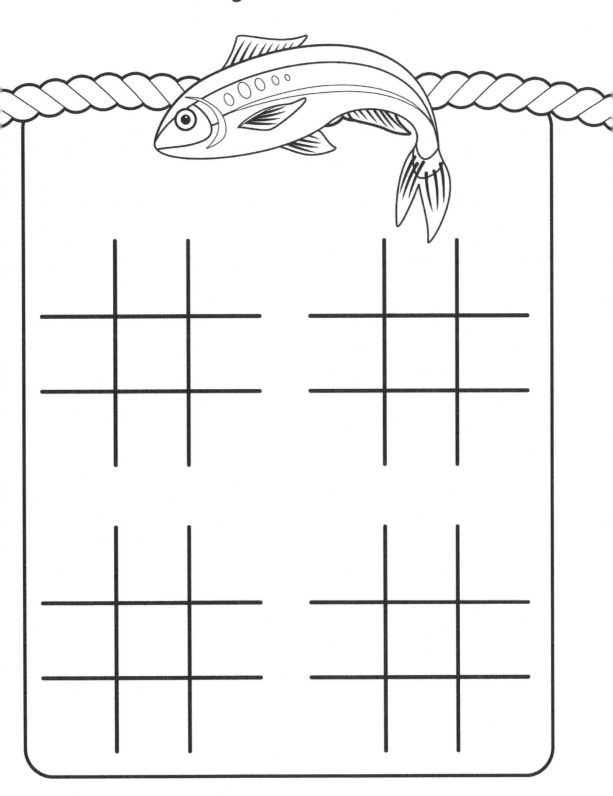

# 🐟 ABOUT MY FISHING TRIP 🐟

Date:_____

Where was it at? _____

Who did you go with?_____

How long did you fish? _____

What was the weather like? _____

How many fish did you catch?_____

What was your favorite part of the trip? _____

_____

_____

What was your least favorite part? _____

_____

_____

DRAW A PICTURE OF SOMETHING FROM YOUR TRIP:

# ABOUT MY FISHING TRIP

Date:_____

Where was it at? _____

Who did you go with?_____

How long did you fish? _____

What was the weather like? _____

How many fish did you catch?_____

What was your favorite part of the trip? _____
_____
_____

What was your least favorite part? _____
_____
_____

**FUN FISHING FACT:**
DESPITE THEIR HORSEY SHAPE, SEA HORSES ARE FISH. THEY HAVE VERY SMALL FINS AND CAN'T SWIM FAST.

DRAW A PICTURE OF SOMETHING FROM YOUR TRIP:

# ABOUT MY FISHING TRIP

Date:_____

Where was it at? _____

Who did you go with?_____

How long did you fish? _____

What was the weather like? _____

How many fish did you catch?_____

What was your favorite part of the trip? _____

_____

_____

What was your least favorite part? _____

_____

_____

# DRAW A PICTURE OF SOMETHING FROM YOUR TRIP:

# COLOR IN THE FISH SCALE PATTERN!

# COLOR IN THE PICTURE!

# ⟨≬⟩ ABOUT MY FISHING TRIP ⟨≬⟩

Date:_____

Where was it at? _____

Who did you go with?_____

How long did you fish? _____

What was the weather like? _____

How many fish did you catch?_____

What was your favorite part of the trip? _____

_____

_____

What was your least favorite part? _____

_____

_____

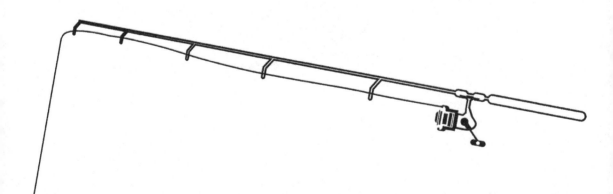

# DRAW A PICTURE OF SOMETHING FROM YOUR TRIP:

#  ABOUT MY FISHING TRIP

Date:_____

Where was it at? _____

Who did you go with?_____

How long did you fish? _____

What was the weather like? _____

How many fish did you catch?_____

What was your favorite part of the trip? _____

_____

_____

What was your least favorite part? _____

_____

_____

FUN FISHING FACT:
FISH ARE COVERED IN SCALES WHICH ARE OFTEN COVERED IN A LAYER OF SLIME TO HELP THEIR MOVEMENT THROUGH WATER.

DRAW A PICTURE OF SOMETHING FROM YOUR TRIP:

# ABOUT MY FISHING TRIP

Date:_____

Where was it at? _____

Who did you go with?_____

How long did you fish? _____

What was the weather like? _____

How many fish did you catch?_____

What was your favorite part of the trip? _____

_____

_____

What was your least favorite part? _____

_____

_____

DRAW A PICTURE OF SOMETHING FROM YOUR TRIP:

# COLOR IN THE FISHING LURES!

# FISH WORD SEARCH
## Find all the listed words!

```
l  w  o  r  m  s  l  c  f  t  s  m  w  a  f
l  h  c  t  r  o  u  t  r  i  s  r  o  a  m
b  e  e  i  r  c  e  h  l  g  i  c  f  n  l
a  f  m  f  l  o  u  n  d  e  r  a  n  u  i
o  n  a  s  a  l  m  o  n  r  p  t  i  t  y
u  s  h  a  h  e  e  r  r  m  m  f  m  o  n
n  p  r  p  c  e  t  a  u  s  f  i  a  n  y
a  e  r  f  i  s  h  i  n  s  c  s  u  i  a
e  a  l  y  m  i  r  n  h  a  e  h  o  s  n
c  l  s  h  e  a  l  e  g  y  n  l  n  e  g
h  p  w  d  u  m  f  l  l  i  a  u  f  l  l
o  a  a  q  o  o  i  s  l  t  l  o  m  a  e
g  w  a  t  e  r  n  m  c  r  r  l  t  c  r
l  n  r  a  n  n  s  y  t  a  n  o  s  s  e
a  u  g  v  n  a  a  t  b  o  w  l  l  o  t
```

| | |
|---|---|
| Fish | Aquarium |
| Bowl | Water |
| Scales | Gills |
| Salmon | Carp |
| Fins | Catfish |
| Tuna | Trout |
| Flounder | Angler |
| Worms | |

# ⌖ ABOUT MY FISHING TRIP ⌖

Date:_____

Where was it at? _____

Who did you go with?_____

How long did you fish? _____

What was the weather like? _____

How many fish did you catch?_____

What was your favorite part of the trip? _____

_____

_____

What was your least favorite part? _____

_____

_____

# DRAW A PICTURE OF SOMETHING FROM YOUR TRIP:

# ABOUT MY FISHING TRIP

Date:_____

Where was it at? _____

Who did you go with?_____

How long did you fish? _____

What was the weather like? _____

How many fish did you catch?_____

What was your favorite part of the trip? _____

_____

_____

What was your least favorite part? _____

_____

_____

FUN FISHING FACT:

OVER 1000 FISH SPECIES ARE THREATENED BY EXTINCTION. FISH RESPONSIBLY!

# DRAW A PICTURE OF SOMETHING FROM YOUR TRIP:

# ABOUT MY FISHING TRIP

Date:_____

Where was it at? _____

Who did you go with?_____

How long did you fish? _____

What was the weather like? _____

How many fish did you catch?_____

What was your favorite part of the trip? _____

_____

_____

What was your least favorite part? _____

_____

_____

DRAW A PICTURE OF SOMETHING FROM YOUR TRIP:

## DID YOU KNOW?

Did you know that flying fish exist? Draw a picture of what you think one looks like, then have an adult look up a picture of a real one online to compare!

COLOR IN THE PICTURE!

# ABOUT MY FISHING TRIP

Date:_____

Where was it at? _____

Who did you go with?_____

How long did you fish? _____

What was the weather like? _____

How many fish did you catch?_____

What was your favorite part of the trip? _____

_____

_____

What was your least favorite part? _____

_____

_____

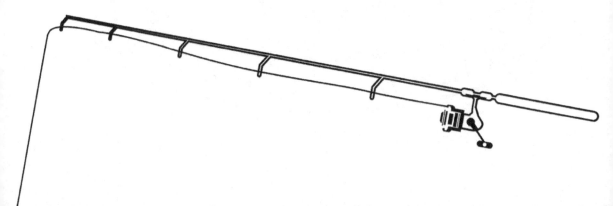

DRAW A PICTURE OF SOMETHING FROM YOUR TRIP:

# ⋈⋉ ABOUT MY FISHING TRIP ⋊⋈

Date:_____

Where was it at? _____

Who did you go with?_____

How long did you fish? _____

What was the weather like? _____

How many fish did you catch?_____

What was your favorite part of the trip? _____

_____

_____

What was your least favorite part? _____

_____

_____

FUN FISHING FACT:
ALTHOUGH CRAYFISH HAVE THE WORD
'FISH' IN THEIR NAME, THEY AREN'T
ACTUALLY FISH. THEY ARE CRUSTACEANS.

DRAW A PICTURE OF SOMETHING FROM YOUR TRIP:

# ⋈⟨⟩ ABOUT MY FISHING TRIP ⟨⟩⋈

Date:_____

Where was it at? _____

Who did you go with?_____

How long did you fish? _____

What was the weather like? _____

How many fish did you catch?_____

What was your favorite part of the trip? _____

_____

_____

What was your least favorite part? _____

_____

_____

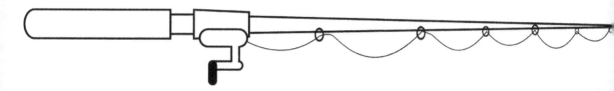

DRAW A PICTURE OF SOMETHING FROM YOUR TRIP:

# FINISH DRAWING THE FISH!
## Get as silly and creative as you want!

# COLOR IN THE PICTURE!

# 🐟 ABOUT MY FISHING TRIP 🐟

Date:_____

Where was it at? _____

Who did you go with?_____

How long did you fish? _____

What was the weather like? _____

How many fish did you catch?_____

What was your favorite part of the trip? _____

_____

_____

What was your least favorite part? _____

_____

_____

# DRAW A PICTURE OF SOMETHING FROM YOUR TRIP:

# ⋈ ABOUT MY FISHING TRIP ⋈

Date:_____

Where was it at? _____

Who did you go with?_____

How long did you fish? _____

What was the weather like? _____

How many fish did you catch?_____

What was your favorite part of the trip? _____

_____

_____

What was your least favorite part? _____

_____

_____

**FUN FISHING FACT:**
FISH ARE ONE OF THE OLDEST ANIMAL
FAMILIES ON EARTH. THEY WERE HERE
500 MILLION YEARS AGO, LONGER THAN
THE DINOSAURS!

DRAW A PICTURE OF SOMETHING FROM YOUR TRIP:

# ABOUT MY FISHING TRIP

Date: _____

Where was it at? _____

Who did you go with? _____

How long did you fish? _____

What was the weather like? _____

How many fish did you catch? _____

What was your favorite part of the trip? _____
_____
_____

What was your least favorite part? _____
_____
_____

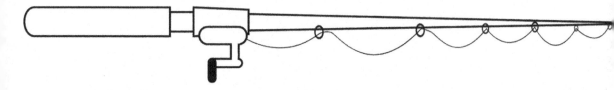

DRAW A PICTURE OF SOMETHING FROM YOUR TRIP:

# COLOR IN THE PICTURE!

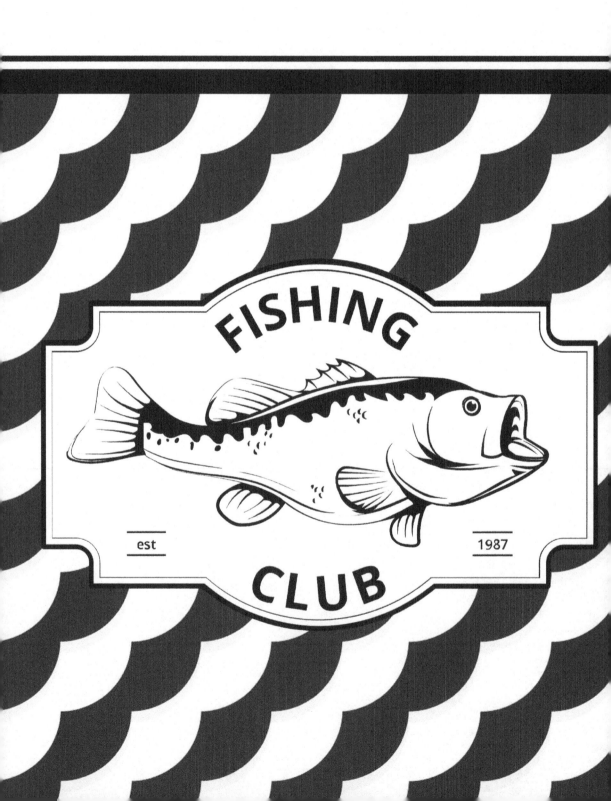

# COLOR IN THE PICTURE!

# 🐟 ABOUT MY FISHING TRIP 🐟

Date:_____

Where was it at? _____

Who did you go with?_____

How long did you fish? _____

What was the weather like? _____

How many fish did you catch?_____

What was your favorite part of the trip? _____

_____

_____

What was your least favorite part? _____

_____

_____

DRAW A PICTURE OF SOMETHING FROM YOUR TRIP:

# 🐟 ABOUT MY FISHING TRIP 🐟

Date:_____

Where was it at? _____

Who did you go with?_____

How long did you fish? _____

What was the weather like? _____

How many fish did you catch?_____

What was your favorite part of the trip? _____

_____

_____

What was your least favorite part? _____

_____

_____

**FUN FISHING FACT:**
SOME FISH LIVE IN SALT WATER, SUCH AS HALIBUT AND COD. THEY LIVE IN OCEANS AND SEAS. FRESHWATER FISH, SUCH AS TROUT AND CATFISH, LIVE IN LAKES AND RIVERS.

DRAW A PICTURE OF SOMETHING FROM YOUR TRIP:

# ABOUT MY FISHING TRIP

Date: _____

Where was it at? _____

Who did you go with? _____

How long did you fish? _____

What was the weather like? _____

How many fish did you catch? _____

What was your favorite part of the trip? _____

_____

_____

What was your least favorite part? _____

_____

_____

# DRAW A PICTURE OF SOMETHING FROM YOUR TRIP:

# COLOR IN THE PICTURE!

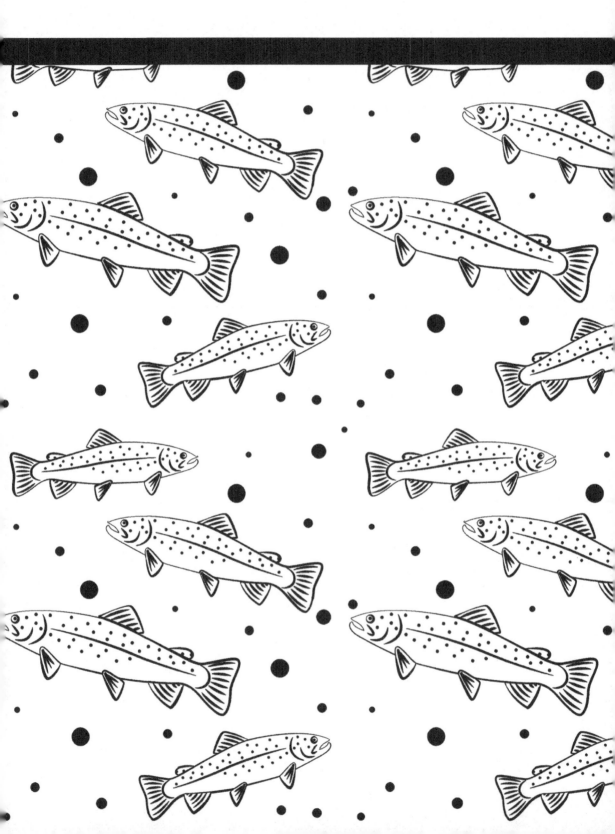

# HELP THE FISH GET BACK TO HIS FRIENDS!

START

FINISH

# ◁≋▷ ABOUT MY FISHING TRIP ◁≋▷

Date:_____

Where was it at? _____

Who did you go with?_____

How long did you fish? _____

What was the weather like? _____

How many fish did you catch?_____

What was your favorite part of the trip? _____

_____

_____

What was your least favorite part? _____

_____

_____

DRAW A PICTURE OF SOMETHING FROM YOUR TRIP:

# ⟅ ABOUT MY FISHING TRIP ⟆

Date:_____

Where was it at? _____

Who did you go with?_____

How long did you fish? _____

What was the weather like? _____

How many fish did you catch?_____

What was your favorite part of the trip? _____

_____

_____

What was your least favorite part? _____

_____

_____

**FUN FISHING FACT:**
THE LARGEST FISH IS THE GREAT WHALE
SHARK. IT CAN GROW TO 50 FEET LONG.
THE TINY PHILIPPINE GOBY IS ABOUT THE
SIZE OF YOUR PINKY FINGERNAIL.

DRAW A PICTURE OF SOMETHING FROM YOUR TRIP:

# ABOUT MY FISHING TRIP

Date:_____

Where was it at? _____

Who did you go with?_____

How long did you fish? _____

What was the weather like? _____

How many fish did you catch?_____

What was your favorite part of the trip? _____

_____

_____

What was your least favorite part? _____

_____

_____

# DRAW A PICTURE OF SOMETHING FROM YOUR TRIP:

# COLOR IN THE PICTURE!

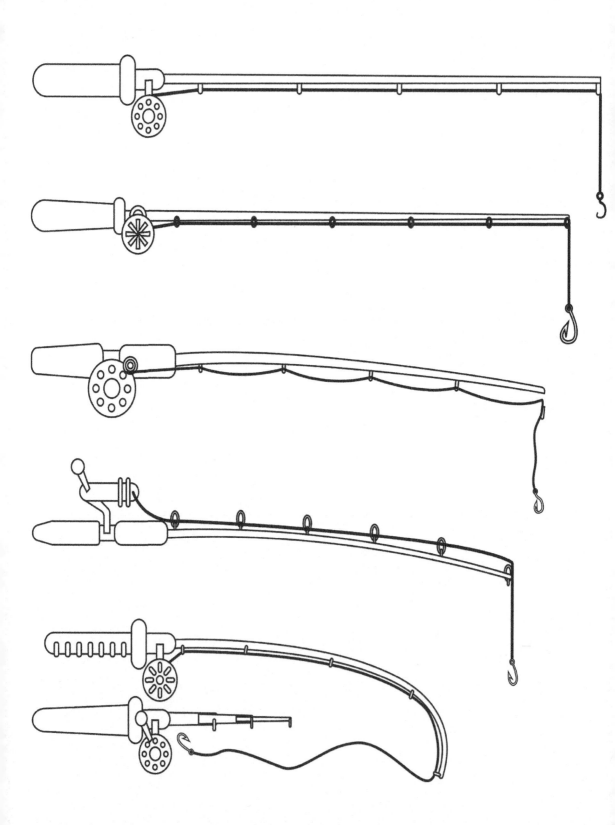

# COLOR IN THE PICTURE!

# ⋈ ABOUT MY FISHING TRIP ⋈

Date:_____

Where was it at? _____

Who did you go with?_____

How long did you fish? _____

What was the weather like? _____

How many fish did you catch?_____

What was your favorite part of the trip? _____

_____

_____

What was your least favorite part? _____

_____

_____

DRAW A PICTURE OF SOMETHING FROM YOUR TRIP:

# ABOUT MY FISHING TRIP

Date:_____

Where was it at? _____

Who did you go with?_____

How long did you fish? _____

What was the weather like? _____

How many fish did you catch?_____

What was your favorite part of the trip? _____

_____

_____

What was your least favorite part? _____

_____

_____

**FUN FISHING FACT:**
FISH CAN BE FOUND ALMOST ANYWHERE THERE ARE BODIES OF WATER. THEY CAN LIVE HIGH UP IN MOUNTAIN STREAMS ALL THE WAY DOWN TO SOME OF THE DEEPEST PARTS OF THE OCEAN.

DRAW A PICTURE OF SOMETHING FROM YOUR TRIP:

# ABOUT MY FISHING TRIP

Date:_____

Where was it at? _____

Who did you go with?_____

How long did you fish? _____

What was the weather like? _____

How many fish did you catch?_____

What was your favorite part of the trip? _____

_____

_____

What was your least favorite part? _____

_____

_____

DRAW A PICTURE OF SOMETHING FROM YOUR TRIP:

Made in the USA
Middletown, DE
27 August 2020